GW00676302

PETER JONES
Solar Wind

Paper Tiger

A Dragon's World Ltd. Imprint

Dragon's World Ltd.,
Limpsfield,
Surrey RH8 0DY,
Great Britain.

Produced by Magnetic Storm Ltd., for Dragon's World Ltd.

ISBN: 0 905895 55 X

Printed in Singapore

To, Robert Spearman.
Many thanks for everything.

Acknowledgements
With special thanks to Cath,
Reg and Debbie for all their
help and encouragement
with my work.

Contents

48	Stardance	Futura	1979
49	Phoenix Without Ashes	Granada	1976
50	The Wizard of Anharitte	Granada	1974
51	Menace Of The Mutant Master (Perry Rhodan)	Futura	1976
52	Vermilion Sands	Granada	1975
53	The Quest Of The D.N.A. Cowboys	Granada	1975
54	Mutants	Transworld	1976
55	The Godmakers	Born	1977
56	Orphans Of The Sky	Granada	1974
57	Clans Of The Alphane Moon	Granada	1974
58	Claws Of Death	Sphere	1976
59	The Venus Trap (Perry Rhodan)	Futura	1976
60/61	Lord Tedric	W.H. Allen	1977
62 T	Beyond The Barrier	Hamlyn	1978
62 B	All My Sins Remembered	Futura	1978
63 T	Infinite Dreams	Futura	1978
63 B	A World Out Of Time	Futura	1978
64 T	The World Of Ptavvs	Futura	1977
64 B	Protector	Futura	1978
65 T	Ox	Transworld	1976
65 B	Omnivore	Transworld	1976
66/67	Phssthpok	Dragon's World	1980
69	Strike Carrier	Dutch Navy	1978
70 TL	Timesnake & Superclown	Futura	1975
70 TR	Stranglers Moon	Granada	1976
70 BL	The Space Merchants	Born	1977
70 BR	The Man Who Awoke	Sphere	1977
71 TL	Buy Jupiter	Granada	1975
71 TR	The Night Watch	Futura	1976
71 BL	The Best of Robert "E" Silverberg	Futura	1975
71 BR	Today We Choose Faces	Futura	1975
72 TL	Rogue Ship	Granada	1975
72 TR	The Imperial Stars	Granada	1975
72 BL	Nebula Award Stories 7 (Nebula 7)	Granada	1974
72 BR	The Centauri Device	Granada	1974
73 TL	The Gold At The Starbow's End	Granada	1974
73 TR	The Chalk Giants	Born	1977
73 BL	The Primitive	Futura	1977
73 BR	The Undercover Aliens	Granada	1975
74	Escape To Venus (Perry Rhodan)	Futura	1975
75	To Here And The Easel	Granada	1974
76	Berserkers Planet/Brother Berserker	Futura	1974
77	The Zap Gun	Granada	1974
78	To Ride Pegasus	Sphere	1977
79	Firestorm	Born	1977
81	Neural Atrocity	Granada	1976
82/83	New Eden	Solar Wind	1979
84 T	Deep Space	Transworld	1976
84 B	The Silent Invaders	Hamlyn	1978
85	Ring Around The Sun	Born	1975
85	Tyranopolis	Sphere	1977
86/87	Interface, Volteface, Multiface	Futura	1977
88/89	Mercenary	Futura	1979
90 T	A Gift From Earth	Futura	1977
90 B	Titan	Futura	1979
91 T	Space Pirates (Lord) Tedric II)	W.H. Allen	1978
91 B	Colony Ship	Solar Wind	1979
92 T	In The Ocean Of Night	Futura	1978
92 B	Telempath	Futura	1978

Biography

'Solar Wind' is a collection of pictures produced between 1974 and 1980. During this time Peter Jones took an interest in science fiction and fantasy, using available imagery to explore many of his own interests, including visual dynamics, fashion, logo design, and anatomical invention.

During his last years at school, he had the good fortune to meet Robert Spearman who encouraged and assisted his progress. Because of him, he went to St. Martin's School of Art, London, from 1971 to 1974.

While in his second year studying Graphics he became interested in the novels of Larry Niven and Isaac Asimov. Subsequently he started to make imagery which had a "sci-fi" feel to it.

A tutor at St. Martin's was very taken with a small painting he had made of a chimpanzee. He thought that Puffin, the publisher of children's books, might be interested. So he went to see them. They had just published their books on wildlife, and there were no further books of that kind to be commissioned for some time to come. However, they were publishing some science fiction. This was his real interest, and he accepted two commissions for paperback covers.

In late 1973 a college friend suggested that he went to see a man at Foyles, the London bookshop. At that time he was receiving encouragement and constructive criticism from two tutors at college. His interest in science fiction grew. He spent hours in book shops studying the composition of paperback covers. The man in Foyles showed his portfolio to a Granada Publishing sales representative who then showed it to his Company's Art Director.

This book is the rest of the story.

"Where Do You Get Your Ideas?"—
"How Do You Get There?"

There is no creative supermarket, no bazaar of the bizarre, open to artists alone, and the space-shuttle hasn't yet started scheduled flights. Peter Jones hasn't run into many accredited aliens (he assumes), and doesn't drive a zero-gravity car. In fact, he doesn't drive at all.

But he can relate his work to the world we all inhabit. "The sheen of a certain shape of car body excites me—or the lack of it, as in a matt-black Porsche. A lot of the impact in illustrated science-fiction hardware stems from our obsession with gleaming metal and glass—perhaps more than from surrealist paintings, or nuclear physics."

His small studio, in a Victorian terrace in South London, supplies more clues to the content of his work. A sinuous Chinese incense burner lies on the desk; pinned to the wall are reproductions of Japanese prints, album covers featuring Chinese script, colour plans of camouflaged fighter planes—all sources for alien body-suits, architecture and space galleons. He mentions Oriental musical instruments as inspirational artefacts: "odd shapes, extraordinary tonal scales, objects that help to suggest 'the alien' for a modern European."

These sources flow into one main reservoir of imagery. Peter Jones' work is a gleeful exploration of the classic stereotypes of 'The Golden

8

Age of Science Fiction' — the period when *'Astounding Stories', 'Startling Stories', 'Amazing Stories',* cheap pulp magazines of 'scientifiction', flashed out in garish pinks and yellows, 1930's fantasies of megacities, cast-iron robots and monstrous startlet-grabbing aliens.

Jones' achievement is this: he has taken the clichés and genres of pulp sci-fi imagery and refined them, inverted them, even extended them. The odd thing is that by manipulating the styles of the past, Jones has stimulated our current expectations, producing a slick couture for weaponry; even ballet costumes for space-station dwellers. There are industrial designers working now on prototypical cars, trains and aeroplanes whose primary inspiration might well have been 'The Zap Gun' (p.77).

Technique

> "No, no! the adventures first,"
> Said the Gryphon in an impatient tone:
> "Explanations take such a dreadful time."

The immediately distinctive aspect of a Peter Jones painting is the subtlety of tone and surface effect even when dealing in the most strident colour combinations. Frank R. Paul's future cities and alien landscapes coloured in pure acid pastel; lime-yellow, raspberry red, blackberry blue. Jones has taken up these colour schemes, but uses every combination of the techniques available to the oil-painter to mellow fabrics, harden metallic edges, coarsen the texture of rock or sand-dune.

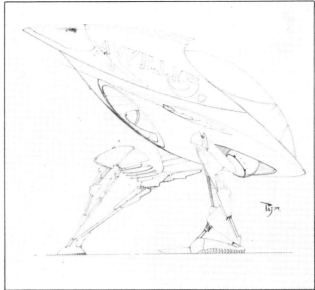

The same refinement is applied to the styling of stock 1950's science-fiction imagery. In 'The Birth Grave' (p.17) 'pulp' colouring enlivens shapes and symbols derived from post-war Hollywood space extravaganzas. The same combination appears throughout this book ('All My Sins Remembered', p.62, 'To Ride Pegasus', p.78).

The training which Peter Jones undertook at college has much to do with this sensitivity. He arrived with a good knowledge of colour theory. A teacher at school, Robert Spearman, had encouraged him to grind his own pigments, perform endless colour chart experiments, paint still lifes composed entirely of white objects, sometimes placed behind a fine gauze screen. He learned how to use tempera and glazes of oil paint before he started his art school course. What he describes as a 'bombardment of imagery with Italian names attached' was his introduction to art history, but perhaps because of the intensity of his training in technique, he rejected 'fine art' at college, and opted for fashion.

The designs he came up with were impractical—"steel suits went out in the Middle Ages," and so he had a brief flirtation with industrial design. Eventually, he decided to study Graphic Design, and extended his interest in military hardware illustration by doodling spacecraft. At the same time, he sketched out animal subjects which he later developed in his paintings of aliens and subhuman life forms.

When Jones started to paint covers for science fiction, he was told by art-directors, "Give me a Foss—any Foss." Though the first cover he did was a futuristic long–ship thundering through rough seas ('King Kobold' p.32), Jones, like most of his contemporaries, went through a period when his pictures were Foss look-alikes. 'Device' (p.72) features a vast, flaky yellow spaceship, with thousands of panels riveted together

into improbable fins, fighter wings and jet manifolds. In other pictures ('The Chalk Giants' p.16) particular contribution to British Sci-Fi imagery was taking shape.

A Note on Technique

Peter Jones says, "Effect supersedes stability". He uses acrylic oil paint. In 'A Canticle For Liebowitz' (pp. 26-27), the dull colours in the background are painted in acrylic; the highlights in the bishop's mitre, and the stained-glass windows of the ecclesiastical spaceship are built up with touches of oil paint. In 'Orn' (pp. 38-39), the colours in the sea, and on the monster, are composed of thin glazes of 'Alkid' oil paint, which dries matt. The cloud textures are brought out by the use of a wax-based varnish, which is sealed-in with another varnish. The sea-splash is attained by flicking light washes of oil paint over the acrylic sky. Most of the 'alien' pictures have acrylic landscape and sky, main characters highlighted in oil. Now and then, Jones uses mixtures of oil and water-based pigment to produce a 'scarred' effect. The nebulous, bubbled alien force in the sky of 'Ox' (p.71), is effected by dropping oil paint onto a layer of clear water on an oil-based background. The majority of the images in this book are painted on hardboard. Where a rough texture, such as rock or sand, was required, the texture of the board has been allowed to show through thin washes of colour. Indeed, some of the sandscapes in this book are painted with a mixture of oil and sand. But in all cases, Jones' intention is to achieve effects which will be reproduced well. Such mixed media can result in fragile artwork. A colour transparency is often the final product.

Sword & Sorcery, Romance & The East

Argument still rattles over the psychological and literary roots of modern science fiction. Some people claim that the decline of organised religion has left a void in modern man's make-up. Notions of immortality have been replaced by fantasies of cloning and time-travel; deities and demons have been transmogrified into Galactic galleon commanders and aliens —or so the argument runs. Another view is that science fiction has always been written: it has been called legend, romance, metaphysical poetry, the Gothic novel, utopian or dystopian projection. Icarus was a form of space man, and is Frankenstein a robot? Unaware of Isaac Asimov's well-considered workshop rules.

The common ingredient of both theories is that the all-powerful spirit or magician has been replaced by the super technologist, the Faust who negotiates with atoms. Magic becomes the time machine or dematerialising ray; computer becomes god.

The truth is that science fiction, like any fiction, cannot help drawing on the conventions of the past. The writers do it; the illustrators do it. The genre which most self-consciously plays on historic forms and symbolism is often called 'sword-and-sorcery' or 'fantasy' to differentiate it from some imagined 'scientific' fiction. But in Peter Jones' 'sword-and-sorcery' work we see how pointless all these distinctions are. Arabian Nights and ion-drive starships, angels, wizards and time-warps, all combine quite comfortably. His illustration for 'The Dark Twin' (p.16, top right) might easily feature Venusians and time travellers, but the subjects are wizard-taught Celtic princes, doomed to the fulfilment of their 'geist' or symbolic destiny. Jones' breakthrough in 1970's British science fiction imagery was to resurrect the genres of romance and oriental gothic.

17

Leviathans

Even when the reference is to the heavyweights of earth's past, the dinosaurs, Jones cannot resist the temptation to mix metaphors. Why should the chorus-girl with her flamingo pet be surprised when the emerging monster turns on her? ('Orn', pp.38-39). Come to that, why a flamingo for a pet? The frontispiece of this book is a succinct statement of Jones' pictorial reasoning. If Brian Aldiss' definition of science-fiction — "Hubris clobbered by Nemesis" is correct, hubris can be a flamingo, a rocket ship or a crayfish, nemesis a dinosaur, a sentient fir-cone, or a battle-suited primitive.

Perhaps the best example in this book of unlikely qualities held together in one image, is the timid alien in 'Neutron Star' (p.31). This mixture of Road Runner, Donald Duck and ostrich, is a member of a species which, though highly intelligent, eschews all contact with any decision of any kind, especially those involving aggression. Alien?

The Alien Corn Aliens, Couples and other Monsters

Geeks, demons and bug-eyed monsters were the order of the editors in the 1930's, 40's and 50's. Rapacious, even when sporting angel wings, the aliens always seemed to win the girl — on the cover of the magazines at least. Aliens could be gorilla-like, made of coiled metal, or look as if they had been dredged up from a sewage works — but the formula remained the same. Girl screamed then swooned, pale breasts straining against a bodice made of heavy duty rice paper. In his most influential pictures, Peter Jones takes the stereotype and switches it completely. Fur-strewn Amazons ('The Female Man', p.46) tower over Caliban-esque pets, who, with their leather collars, and the leads, crouch punk-like in the dirt where they belong. Or a beautiful girl's head is seen nestling against the neck-plate of a wizened time-lord ('Clans Of The Alphane Moon', p.57). The same reversal is applied to the alien landscapes and machines in Jones' pictures. Can that be a galactic cabbage the bikini-clad princess poses under in 'The Killer Mice' (p.47)? and is that horrible alien fighting machine really composed of a crayfish's legs, a turtle-shell radar dome, and a half-peeled potato ('Ox', p65).

The answer: they are but they aren't. Through a witty dislocation of visual language, Jones' imagery conveys surprise and impact. Expectations are jangled. No pitted, cratered landscapes on many of his alien worlds. Instead, unremarkable specimens from earth's natural history mixed and magnified into strangeness.

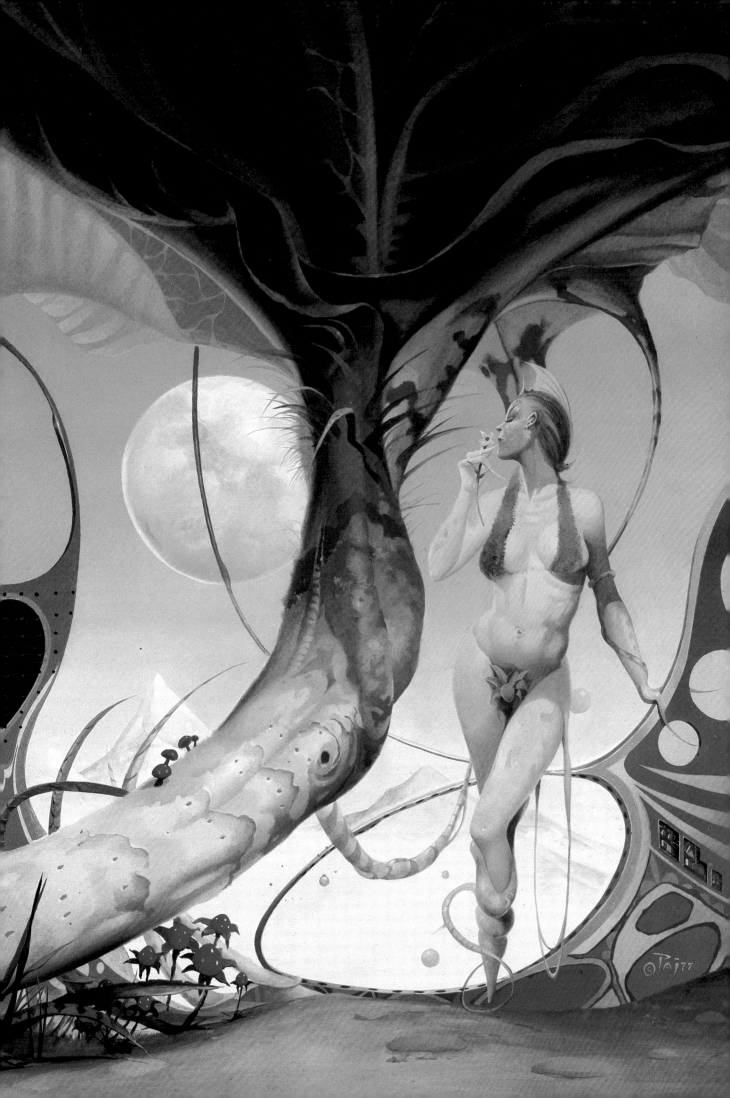

All The Worlds Are Stages

The possibilities in architectural form, landscape and style of civilization in fantasy and science-fiction are limitless. Peter Jones' interest in fashion design has been extended into the creation of elaborate sets within which characters move like dancers on a stage. (His wife, Deborah, is a trained ballet dancer). 'The Killer Mice' (p.47) was one of the first pictures in which elegant backdrops, related to nothing but the overall design of a picture, appear. In later pictures, the settings evoke atmosphere more precisely. In 'Infinite Dreams' (p.63), a 'true romance' setting—beach, palm trees and lovers—is rudely shattered by the appearance of an alien in a corset-shaped time capsule. In this picture, images clash, the result of careful stage-management. In others, the sense of a co-ordinated film set is achieved—costume, machines and landscape carefully tailored to each other—especially in 'Interface' (pp. 86-87) which looks like a 'still' taken from a huge movie project.

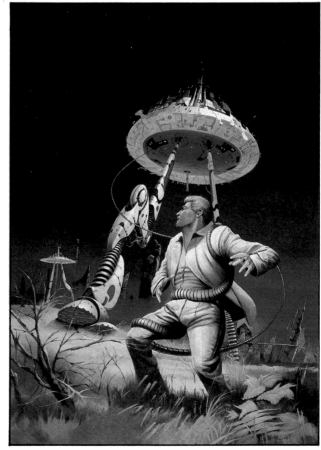

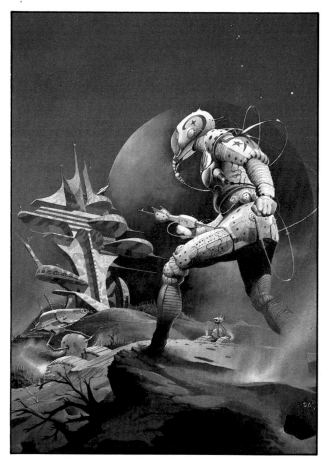

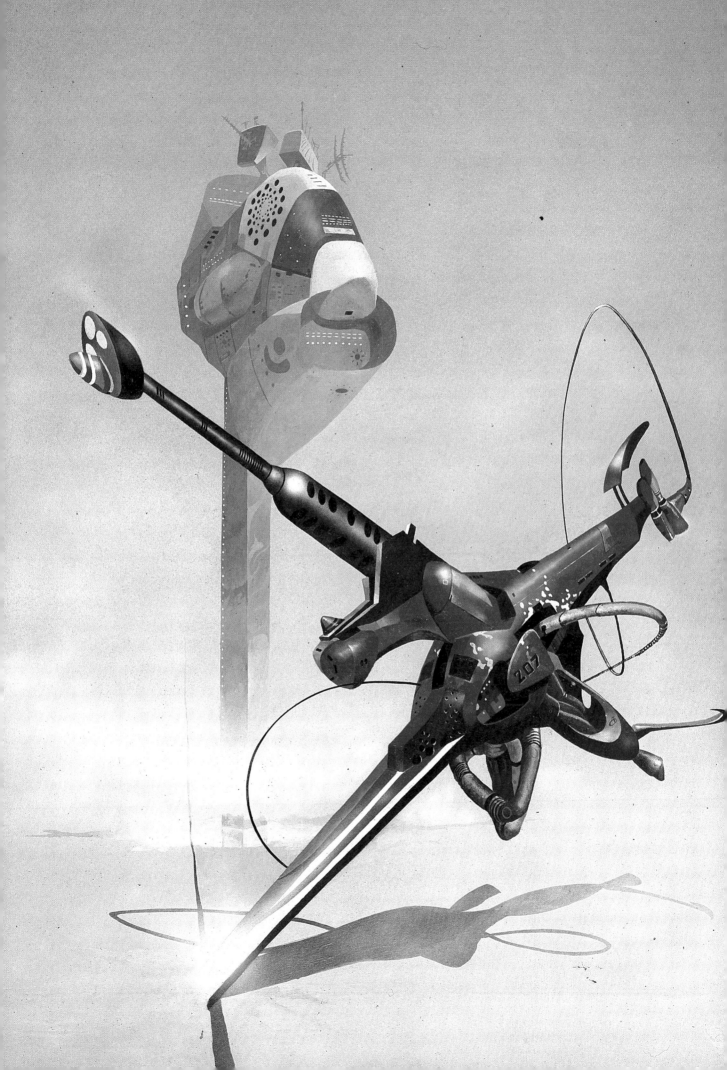

Life Imitating Art

Peter Jones' work now extends 'film sets' into reality. He works out the interiors of his space craft very carefully, the graphics on the consoles, the upholstery of the pod-shaped seating, the curves of rails and in-ship machinery. In 'The Silent Invaders' and 'Deep Space' (p.84), this detailing is put at the service of book-jacket designs, but in 'New Eden' (pp.82-83), Jones has painted a picture to his own specifications. As in 'The Zap Gun' (p.77), the power of the image stems from the fact that it is impossible to name the function of its constituents. Is the spiky green object in the left foreground a sculpture, an oxygenation plant, or some form of monitoring device? And what about the new-wave space dwellers, with purple hair and body paint? Are they controlled by the floating machine to which they are connected by tendrils? These questions are left unanswered. Peter Jones says with a grin, "I like this picture because I don't know what's happening in it!" Questioned about his future ambitions, Jones says that product design might be of major interest to him, anything from cars to spaceships. Who can tell?

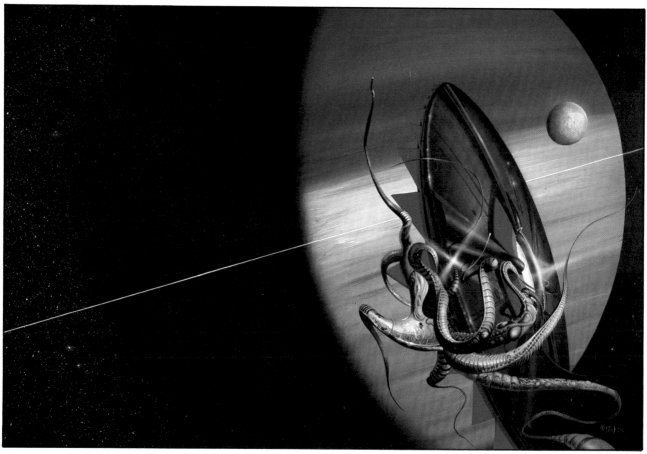